THE BIG DUCK

Written by Linda Trott Dickman

Illustrated by Long Island "Ducklings" from Northport High School, Robin O'Neill-Gonzalez's Studio in Crafts Class

Photos by Jennifer N. Frey

Lily Suarez

Cover art by: Maddy Solloch

Copyright © 2025
All rights reserved.
Published by Red Penguin Books
Bellerose Village, New York
ISBN 978-1-63777-644-5 | 978-1-63777-709-1
No part of this book may be reproduced in any form or by any electronic or mechanical means, including information storage and retrieval systems, without written permission from the author, except for the use of brief quotations in a book review.

For all those who herd, plant, teach, draw and write.
For lovers of history, and those who make it.
Linda Trott Dickman

Hailey Seemungal

AUTHOR'S NOTE

This big quacker has been a part of my life for a very long time. I visited The Big Duck in every location but the original storefront in Riverhead. There is something about her that says "Welcome" and inspires many different puns, movie references and jokes. I just love her. On my last visit, my daughter and I discovered that there was not one book to be had in the gift shop.

That sent this librarian on a quest. I discovered several books that mentioned her, and one that was actually about her. Sadly it was not for sale in the gift shop. This one was inspired by the Big Duck and the many students I taught over the years. I have virtually traveled all over the Eastern Seaboard and to Arizona in search of information about her, her designers.

This first edition features illustrations by Robin O'Neill-Gonzalez's 2023/24 Freshman Class of Northport High School, which is in Suffolk County, (the home of the Big Duck) on Long Island, NY. The photographs were taken by the parent of a former student who also made Long Island her "beat" as a New York State Trooper. Jennifer Natalie Frey supported every project I ever started with the gift of her incredible photography.

Look for future editions to include student artists from Nassau County, the state of New York, and well, who knows?

~ Linda Trott Dickman

Gabriella Andriano

Marleigh Grodinsky

Charlotte Radigan

Martin Maurer had a farm
E I E I O
and on that farm he had some ducks
E I E I O
there were duck ducks here,
there were ducks ducks there
here a duck
there a duck
everywhere a duck duck
Martin Maurer had a farm
E I E I O

Andrew Winiarski

Madeline Mandel

Sutton Strasser

Valerie Velasquez

Annie Jiang

Juele and Martin took a trip
E I E I O
they stopped for coffee, had a sip
E I E I O
with a sip sip here
and a sip sip there
here a sip, there a sip
everywhere a sip, sip
Juele and Martin took a trip
E I E I O

Noelle Tinghtella

Ella Mugno

Martin had a fun idea
E I E I O
To sell more ducks to folks right here
E I E I O
There were duck, ducks here
there were duck, ducks there
here a duck
there a duck
everywhere a duck duck
Martin had a fun idea
E I E I O

Gabriella Andriano

Alyssa Hradek

Gabriella Andriano

Isla McAlister

Emmalie Kutzma

Sutton Strasser

Martin Maurer had some land
E I E I O
He began to hatch a plan
E I E I O
there was land right here
there was land right there
Here some land, there some land
everywhere was ranch land
Martin Maurer had some land
E I E I O

Abby Holbrook

Christina Neems

Christina Keaveny

George Reeve* the craftsman was engaged
E I E I O
two brothers from the Vaudeville stage*
E I E I O
A Collins here
A Collins there
here a man, there a man
everywhere a good plan
George Reeve, the craftsman was engaged
E I E I O

Ava Scheibe

Chloe DeCrescenzo

Alex Molina-Reyes

Brooke Heffernan

Reeve studied bones of fowl for form
E I E I O
the wooden frame primed to adorn
E I E I O
some cement right here,
and some mesh right there
here some paint,
there some paint
white and street-line-orange paint
Martin Maurer had his duck
E I E I O

Audrey DiLorenzo

Ava Scheibe

Lily Suarez

A Model T provided light
E I E I O
So that the Duck was seen at night
E I E I O
Now a nest right here
wait, a nest right there
here a nest,
there a nest
finally the best nest
A Model T provided light
E I E I O

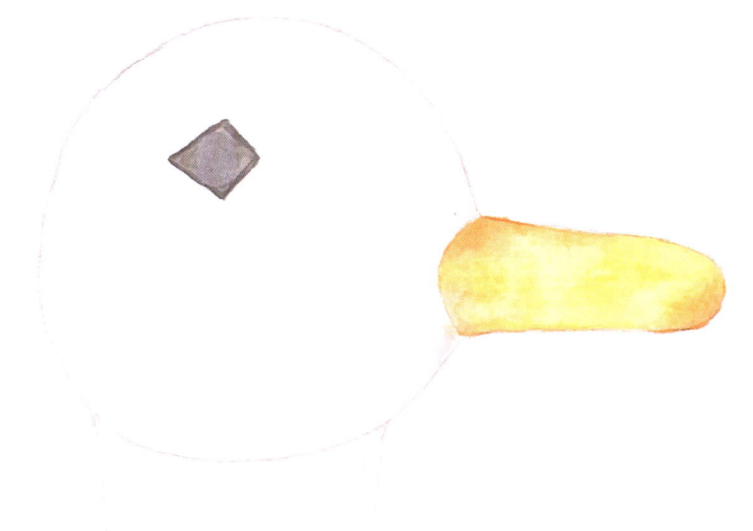

Abby Arabadjief

Emma Murhpy

Martin Maurer's dream took shape
E I E I O
Part of Flanders' pretty 'scape
E I E I O
There are school kids here
There were tourists there
Here a look, there a look
everywhere a good look
Martin Maurer's dream took shape
E I E I O

Charlie O'Brien

Jordan Stewart

Jennifer Natalie Frey

Martin Maurer's Duck still stands
E I E I O
making memories, the plan
E I E I O
Long Island lore
tales by the score
Here a tale
there a tale
everywhere a Duck Tale
Martin Maurer's Duck still stands
E I E I O

Scarlett Hill

Sierra Albano

ACKNOWLEDGMENTS

David L. Dickman
Joanna L. Dickman Courbanou
Janet Clare Fagal
Charles Ghigna
Jennifer N. Frey

BIG DUCK FUN FACTS

Big Coffee Pot building, the "Hot Cha Cafe'" in Long Beach, California inspired Martin Maurer and his wife Jeule, to create a building shaped like what they farmed: ducks.

Interested in boosting sales, Martin commissioned architect George Reeve to construct a new shop.

Grand dimensions - The building stands 30 feet tall and is 18 feet wide. Inside, it's 11×15 feet.

D "duck architecture" to classify any building that was a symbol, that took the shape of its function, became an architectural term.

Uprooted from its original location, the Big Duck moved from Main Street in Riverhead, to the entrance to the Sears Bellows County Park from 1988 to 2007 and back to Flanders on Route 24, in 2007.

Constructed of ferro-cement,* over a wooden frame, the Big Duck structure weighs ten tons.

Kids and their families visit The Big Duck year round. Its most popular seasons are summer and winter, when there is a "Big Duck Lighting" every year.

*definition: a composite structural material comprising thin sections consisting of cement mortar reinforced by a number of closely spaced layers of steel wire mesh.- ACI Concrete Terminology

*William, Samuel and Thomas Collins worked on B.F. Keith's Vaudeville Circuit. There is no mention of any show that they specifically worked on. William was known as a property and set designer. ~ County Review, March 16, 1923

Leila Senra

THANK YOU TO:

- The Billy Rose Theater Division of the New York Public Library
- The Library of Congress, Performing Arts, Music Division, Morgan Davis
- The Emma S, Clark Public Library, Riverhead, Cher Armstrong
- The University of Arizona, Vaudeville Library, David Solon
- The Smithtown Public Library, Long Island Room and their rich resources
- Dr. Susan Van Scoy, author The Big Duck
- Adelphi University Library, Professor Aditi Bandyopadhyay
- The Historic Staunton Foundation, Staunton, VA.

BIBLIOGRAPHY

- Books

The Big Duck and Eastern Long Island's Duck Farming Industry - Dr. Susan Van Scoy. Arcadia Publishing, 2019

Buildings in Disguise - by Joan Marie Arborgast, Boyds Mills Press, 2004

Duckhampton by Christian McLean, illustrated by Amelia Haviland, Duckhamption Press, Flanders, NY, 2006

A Duck's Tale (The Story of a Big Duck and the Small Town that Loves Her) by Rose Nigro, illustrated by Tom H. John. Reeves Bay Artworks, 2008

Alice Le Berre

BIBLIOGRAPHY P. 2

- Periodicals/Websites

The Coffee Pot Building, Long Beach California - Field Team at Roadside America © Copyright 1996-2023 Doug Kirby, Ken Smith, Mike Wilkins. All rights reserved.

Five Things to Know About the Big Duck by Beth Ann Clyde, The Long Island Pulse, 2015

The Big Duck- History
https://aconlan.wixsite.com/the-big-duck/history-of-the-big-duck

Memorializing the Big Duck's Original Roost in Riverhead -Denise Civiletti, Nov. 2020
https://riverheadlocal.com/2020/11/23/memorializing-the-big-ducks-original-roost-in-riverhead/

NY's Cherished Roadside Attraction, Long Island's Big Duck, Is A Train Ride Away

Cam Graziano

RESOURCES FOR ADULTS WORKING WITH CHILDREN

Chickens and More
Pekin Duck All You Need To Know: Care, Eggs and More...

Enchanted Learning
https://www.enchantedlearning.com/search/?f=9&query=Duck&s=r

Super Teacher Work Sheets
https://www.superteacherworksheets.com/sight-words-individual/duck-3_CHIII.pdf

Crescent Duck Farm
Crescent Duck Farm | Farms & Partners | Baldor Specialty Foods

Avery McArdle

HOW YOU CAN HELP

Friends of the Big Duck - an organization that helps preserve the Big Duck.
https://bigduck.org/

Author's Note: We are determined to promote this important part of Long Island's history, and the students who visit The Big Duck, on their way to someplace else, or specifically to experience the Big Duck. Toward that end, subsequent editions will highlight students from all over Long Island. You will be able to find it on Amazon, Barnes & Noble, from Red Penguin Books, and on ShopBooksDirect.com. A portion of the proceeds will go toward helping keep the Big Duck healthy.

ABOUT

About the Author

- Linda Trott Dickman is a dreamer of dreams, a believer in the power of one, a writer who is making a difference. She is a native of Long Island, New York and her spirit is nurtured by pine and leis. A NYS Woman of Distinction, 2023. Let her draw you in, to the crisp air of the mountains, the lush fragrance of the valley, the salty air of the sea, the folds of history's skirts.

About the Photographer

- Jennifer Natalie Frey is a native Long Island Photographer. She served as a New York State Trooper for many years. She lives on the North Shore of Long Island with her family.

About their Teacher

- Robin O'Neill Gonzalez is the enthusiastic, opportunities-for-her-students-seeking, gifted art teacher behind the illustrations that you see featured here. Robin's positive attitude and example say, "Yes you can!" to everyone she encounters. She is a supportive force behind collaborations with local artists, local organizations, and her church family. Her displays, her art, and her students shine with her enthusiasm.

Chloe Reyes

Mrs. O'G's Combined Class Artists

Sierra Albano
Gabriella Andriano
Abigail Arabadjief
Noa Berger
Claudia Buzzell
Kayla Castillo
Lindsay Connolly
Chloe DeCrescenzo
Audrey DiLorenzo
Korienne Fauser
Marley Grodinksy
Cam Graziano
Brooke Heffernan
Scarlett Hill
Abigail Holbrook
Ayssa Hradek
Annie Jiang
Christina Keaveny
Julianna Kelleher
Emmalie Kutzma
Alice Le Berre
Scarlett Levy

Nora Magas
Madline Mandel
Mia Maxwell
Isla McAllister
Avery McArdle
Alexi Molina-Reyes
Graziella Mugno
Emma Murphy
Christina Neems
Charles O'Brien
Charlotte Radigan
Chloe Reyes
Jude Rooney
Hailey Seemungal
Leila Serna
Finn Siravo
Madalynn Solloch
Jordan Stewart
Sutton Strasser
Lily Suarez
Noelle Tinghitella
Valerie Velazquez Maradiaga
Ava Velez-Recher
Andrew Winiarski
Josetta Zwielich

www.ingramcontent.com/pod-product-compliance
Lightning Source LLC
Chambersburg PA
CBRC101521070526
44585CB00010B/176